THE TWO WESLEYS.

A LECTURE

DELIVERED IN

THE METROPOLITAN TABERNACLE LECTURE HALL,

ON DECEMBER 6TH 1861.

BY

C. H. SPURGEON.

WIPF & STOCK · Eugene, Oregon

Wipf and Stock Publishers
199 W 8th Ave, Suite 3
Eugene, OR 97401

The Two Wesleys
On John and Charles Wesley
By Spurgeon, Charles H.
ISBN 13: 978-1-4982-0531-3
Publication date 9/15/2014
Previously published by Alabaster, Passmore, & Sons, 1861

THE TWO WESLEYS.

AST Friday night I announced a subject which is far too extensive for one lecture; in fact, I think that lectures upon "THE COMPANIONS OF WHITEFIELD" would last almost as long as those of my friend Mr. Davies* upon English History. I sent word to the excellent bookseller who generally hunts up for me all the works upon any one subject, and he sent me such a goodly pile of books, that I very soon discovered that I should be embarrassed with having too much matter.

Seeing that John Wesley and his brother were the first "companions of Whitefield", and were entitled to the chief place, I commenced with their lives, intending to give a sort of brief sketch, and then to bring in many others; but I found that the life of John Wesley was quite sufficient for half-a-dozen lectures; for he was a man who did so much, a man who was so incessantly active, that one could not even

---

* Mr. Spurgeon was referring here to the Friday-evening Lectures in connection with the College, to which, during the autumn and winter months of 1861–2, the public were admitted at a nominal charge. The first part of the evening was generally devoted to Lectures on the History of England, by the Rev. Benjamin Davies, the first pastor of the Church in Greenwich, of which the Rev. Charles Spurgeon is now pastor. Mr. Davies died in 1872, in the fortieth year of his age.

give an outline of his life without its taking up a lecture. I have decided, therefore, to take the *two* WESLEYS, and make them the subject of our lecture to-night.

And now, unless I have the happiness of having here very many of those who agree with John Wesley in doctrinal sentiment, I can hardly think that I shall be able to please you. To ultra-Calvinists his name is as abhorrent as the name of the Pope to a Protestant : you have only to speak of Wesley, and every imaginable evil is conjured up before their eyes, and no doom is thought to be sufficiently horrible for such an arch-heretic as he was. I verily believe that there are some who would be glad to rake up his bones from the tomb and burn them, as they did the bones of Wickliffe of old,—men who go so high in doctrine, and withal add so much bitterness and uncharitableness to it, that they cannot imagine that a man can fear God at all unless he believes precisely as they do.

On the other hand, it is quite impossible that I should please the followers of Mr. Wesley. I intend to publish the lecture, and I have no doubt whatever that it will provoke their criticism ; for, unless you can give him constant adulation, unless you are prepared to affirm that he had no faults, and that he had every virtue, even impossible virtues, you cannot possibly satisfy his admirers. It is very truly said that "love is blind" : in many of the followers of Wesley love is doubly blind, and wears over its blindness very often a pad to prevent any light coming in upon the character of that very good man.

Now I, who am neither an Arminian nor a hyper-Calvinist, but a Calvinist of Calvin's own stamp, think I can stand between the two parties. Believing all that the hyper-Calvinist believes, and preaching as high doctrine as ever he can preach, but believing more than he believes ; not believing all the Arminian believes, but still at the same time believing that he is often sounder than the hyper-Calvinist upon some points of doctrine; I venture to take my stand, I think, with an unbiassed spirit. Not thinking enough of Wesley to become a partizan, not thinking so little of him as to become an adversary, I can, perhaps, make a fairly correct sketch of his life.

If I had more time to read through all his works,— which would take, I suppose, a year or so,—if we could read all the lives that have been written of him, and then collate opinions, we might, perhaps, with calm, unbiassed judgment, arrive at something like the truth. At any rate, I flatter myself that I am qualified to make a pretty fair judgment of his character, not being biassed either way, and I have not more egotism in saying this than Mr. John Wesley displays in the preface to his Hymn Book, which is, by the way, the noblest specimen of egotism committed to pen and ink.

You heard last Friday night, in Dr. Campbell's very admirable lecture upon George Whitefield, that there was an intimate connection between the two ; that when Whitefield first went to Oxford, he had little fear of God before his eyes, and little thought of heavenly things. But he found John and Charles Wesley there, and though they could not teach him the gospel, they could impress him with the importance of eternal realities, and they did so ; and very much of his real earnestness about the things of God was due to association with John and Charles. From that time they formed a very intimate friendship with each other; they were co-labourers, working side by side for many years.

When, at last, the controversy sprang up concerning the Arminian and the Calvinistic doctrines, Whitefield conducted his part of the controversy with the kindest and most gracious spirit, and, I think, I may add, Mr. Wesley did the same. They disputed with one another as brethren, not as enemies; and they both, I think, held each other in quite as high esteem when they differed as when they agreed. In proof of this, you will remember that Whitefield chose Mr. Wesley to preach his funeral sermon, and he did preach it in the Tabernacle, and a more loving eulogy upon a godly man could never have been poured forth by one who had perfectly agreed with him. But while Mr. Wesley differed in many very important points, yet he extolled and loved Whitefield from his very soul, and spoke of him as only one could speak who loved and valued that man of God.

As for Whitefield's opinion of Wesley, there is a story current, to the effect that some Calvinist, who was exceedingly wrathful with Mr. Wesley, once said to Mr. Whitefield, "Do you think we shall ever see John Wesley in heaven?" Whitefield stopped, and said, "Do I think we shall ever see John Wesley in heaven? Well, I do not think we shall," said he. So then our friend thought that Mr. Whitefield quite agreed with him in his bitterness. "But," added Mr. Whitefield, "the reason why we shall not see him is this,—I am afraid that you and I will be so far off the throne of Christ, and Wesley will be so near, that he will be lost in the brightness of his Saviour, and I hardly think you and I will be able to see him." Our friend turned away in a moment, having got quite a contrary answer from that which he expected from the lips of George Whitefield.

Now I, who admire Whitefield as much as the Wesleyan admires Wesley, though I am not therefore bound to close my eyes to his faults, think very highly of Wesley because George Whitefield did so, and I should not like to differ from Whitefield in his opinion. In studying the life of Mr. Wesley, I believe Whitefield's opinion is abundantly confirmed—that Wesley is near the eternal throne, having served his Master, albeit with many mistakes and errors, yet from a pure heart, fervently desiring to glorify God upon the earth.

The difference between the two men, as it was hinted

at by Dr. Campbell, might be enlarged upon. Whitefield was impetuous, his was a fiery spirit; Wesley was cool, calculating, nothing could ruffle him: even if he were in a bad temper you could not know it. If he were in the midst of great danger he never for a moment lost his composure, but could look death in the face with unblanched cheek. He could go to meet his greatest adversary, and that adversary would be led to think that Wesley was the subject of no sort of emotion: he was just the man to head a confraternity, because he was able to keep his feelings in thorough subjection.

Whitefield, in his preaching, was an orator, which is something more than Wesley was. Wesley, in his preaching, endeavoured to demonstrate truth with logical precision, but Whitefield carried men's hearts by storm with burning eloquence. Whitefield's force was the force of Richard Cœur de Lion with his battle-axe, cleaving a bar of iron at a blow; Wesley's was the force of Saladin with his keen scimitar, cutting through a muslin handkerchief. He had keenness, Whitefield had force. Each of them was useful in his own way, but Whitefield came down with all the ponderousness of the battle-axe; the other man won his way with all the keenness of the scimitar.

John Wesley looked very much at church polity, he looked to a great extent at the outside of religion. But Whitefield cared very little about policy; in fact, he could not understand it, and did not meddle with it. He had to deal most with the spirit, the vitals of religion, the soul and essence of godliness. Wesley could form the clay, and make it into the vessel; Whitefield could not do that, but he could turn the potter's wheel, he could give forth that force and power by which, through God, the church might afterwards be formed. George Whitefield was a conservative in doctrine, he held by the old truth, the old Assembly's Catechism, the old Articles of the Church. Wesley was a kind of radical, upsetting anything and everything, and yet, strange to say, Wesley was the greatest possible conservative in points of church polity. He was a thorough-going Churchman, while Whitefield, on the other hand, might be considered a radical in polity, not caring a whit about Episcopacy or Presbyterianism, or anything of the kind, not stickling on any of these points. In fact, I think I might say George Whitefield had his eye fixed on heaven, and he read all truth in the light of God, while John Wesley had his eye fixed on man, and with a tear in his eye, weeping over man's fall and ruin, he read truth in the light of his sympathy with man.

That man will just hit the truth, who can read the truth in both ways ; with his eye full of tears, thinking of man ; with his eye gleaming with sunlight, thinking of God ; he who can preach Divine sovereignty, and yet preach human responsibility ; he who can declare that God "hath mercy on whom He will have mercy, and whom He will He hardeneth," and yet with equal vigour can say, " Know ye not that they which run in a race run all, but one receiveth the prize ? "

As for John Wesley's doctrine, I have not an atom of sympathy with him, except so far as he preached the Gospel of Christ. Now, the essential doctrine of the Gospel is justification by faith. " Therefore being justified by faith, we have peace with God through our Lord Jesus Christ." *That* he did preach ; and though on one occasion, as I shall have to show you in his life, there was a sad error in respect to this fundamental doctrine ; yet he and his followers did, and do, as faithfully preach this truth as any denomination of Christians under heaven. It is not true that they preach salvation by works ; at least, we ought to believe what they say ; for they assert again and again and again, that nothing is more loathsome in their estimation than the idea that any man may be saved by his works. They reject the accusation which is brought against them as altogether without foundation, though there was one unhappy instance in which they did assert, though yet it was hardly meant, salvation by the works of the law.

Wesley not only preached justification by faith very clearly, but so he did the total ruin of our race; and, whatever some of his followers may do, he himself did teach the inability of the creature, and that without the Spirit of God nothing can be done. In fact, this was the prominent doctrine of these Methodists, both Calvinistic and Arminian, that everything is of the grace of God, and that conversion is the effect of the Divine influence which emanates from the Holy Ghost. For this they were constantly persecuted, in common with the other Methodists, and it is not fair to charge upon them that they attribute conversion to the creature. They may do so by inference; but, as a matter of statement, they always assert that salvation is of the Holy Spirit, and of the Holy Spirit alone.

The greatest errors, I think, of Wesley's doctrine were, first of all, the doctrine of *sinless perfection*. But even that I cannot quite understand; for I have a sermon of Mr. Wesley's—a Wesleyan brother had the kindness some years ago to make me a present of all Mr. Wesley's works, a very long list indeed, I have the complete set, and have read most of his works and journals;—I say, I cannot understand how he believed it, for there is a sermon of his, upon " Indwelling Sin in Believers ", which exactly expresses the ordinary idea of the Church of Christ.

In this sermon Mr. Wesley says that nobody ever thought that believers were free from sin, till Count Zinzendorf, the Moravian leader, made that wonderful discovery; and he goes on to argue against it with all his usual precision, and thoroughly demolishes the theory that believers can be truly free from sin, declaring that every soul remains in corruption. Still, he did think that at certain seasons, when believers were filled with the Spirit,

they were so filled with love to Christ, and so perfectly
consecrated to Him, that they did for a time abstain from
sin. Not but that they went back again to sin, and that
at other times they were subject to constant falls ; but that
at certain high and noble seasons, when their spirits were
made like the chariots of Ammi-nadib, they were carried
beyond the influence of sin and the world altogether, and
were for that time perfectly free from all thought and act
of sin. Not such a very gross error, to my thinking,
except when he goes on to say, that sometimes they might
continue in that state by the month together, and perhaps
constantly.

I only wish it were true, I certainly wish that I could get
there, and stand upon that mountain-top for ever.   But,
alas, I feel this, that when I have sprung up on high, the
poor flesh has still followed to pull me down again, and
bring me once more to the common level of infirmity, and
weakness, and unbelief, and sin.

Mr. Wesley did not seem inclined utterly to reject *the
doctrine of election* when first he was in fellowship with
Mr. Whitefield ; but after a time he became its most violent
and bitter opponent.   I think he could not have under-
stood it ; he must have misrepresented it, first to his own
mind, and then, having made a man of straw, he hastened
to shoot his arrows against it.   The doctrine of *effectual
calling* was another point upon which I think he was
exceedingly wrong, for he went to the very extreme ; and
as to the doctrine of *final perseverance*, though he said at
first, in order to keep peace with Mr. Whitefield, he was
willing to concede that some believers might come into
such a state as that afterwards they would never fall away
and perish, yet, as a general rule, he thought it was possible
for believers to perish.

His preaching was constantly against the doctrine of
final perseverance, and, I must add, sometimes he preached

with all the ferocious bitterness that any man could be animated with against those great truths of election and final perseverance which are the comfort of our hearts. So far, he finds no apologist in me ; so far, I must loathe the doctrine that he preached. But notwithstanding that the grace of God lives in a man's heart under a thousand errors, and that God may make a man useful, provided he preaches that one truth, justification by faith, though not so useful as he might have been had he been more clearly instructed in the faith ; yet up to the measure in which he preached God's truth, God would own that truth, and souls would be saved. All this you must consider as a preface, if you please, to John Wesley, and now I mean to proceed to his history.

Now I shall need to have another preface ; for I must describe history at large before I can bring John Wesley himself upon the stage. I shall have to take the liberty of bringing his great-grandfather, and his grandfather, and his father and mother before you, before I can introduce the man himself.

When the Church of England was first of all established, it was intended to be a compromise between Rome and Geneva ; the Pope and the Pope's adherents were not to be too much shocked with ultra-Protestantism ; on the other hand, the Calvinists, the followers of the great Genevan divine, were not to be too much shocked with Popery. So the Prayer Book was made, a translation of a Popish mass-book, and into it was put a sufficient quantity of Romish errors to keep in good humour the Popish faction, that is, such as are now called Puseyites : they have always been in it, called under some name or other. *Absolution* was kept in it, *infant baptism* was kept in it, the burial of all the dead *in sure and certain hope*, and such like things ; these were retained so as to keep on good terms with the Papists.

Then there was a Calvinistic Article written—the Articles

are, for the most part, sound enough,—that was to keep the
Calvinists in, so that they might not go away ; and to this
day such good men as Dr. Hooker can remain in the
Church, and justify their being there because they say the
Articles are Calvinistic.   In order to keep in the Arminians,
the Catechism was made Arminian, as well as parts of the
Liturgy.   Then there were some brethren who believed in
immersion, and to keep them in, the word " dip " was
inserted.

Every effort was put forth to make the Church of
England a good and comprehensive system which might
embrace men of all sorts and all creeds.   Unfortunately, it
took in the bad of all sorts, but did not exactly suit the good
of any sort, for the conscientious Romanist said, " No, I
cannot swear by that ; I am a Catholic."   The Calvinist said,
" Well, I love those Articles, but I cannot swallow the
Popery of the Church of England," and consequently the
great Puritan body came out of the Church.

There was also a race of men, Arminians, who stood
prepared to come out of the Church, whose case Wesley
exactly fitted ; men who were prepared to come out, for
they were not contented with the Calvinistic Articles, though
they might be satisfied on other matters.   And mark, if ever
the religion of England wakes up thoroughly, the Church
of England must perish ; there is no help for it, it cannot live.
I do not say that in a spirit of animosity to that Church, for
there are very many godly men in it.   The Church will
not perish, so far as it is the Church of Christ ; but so
far as it is a compromise between truth and error, it cannot
stand ; that is utterly impossible.   The Calvinist will go his
way, the Arminian will go his way, and the Puseyite his way,
and there will be none left.   Anything that is not founded
on the principles of truth, altogether apart from compromise, has in it the elements of weakness.   A house
divided against itself cannot by any possibility stand.

The Calvinists in the Church were for a long time kept under; but at last, being a strong and powerful body, and not understanding then the peace principles of Messrs. Bright and Cobden, they formed a confederation amongst themselves, to take their own cause in hand, and fight it out with the sword. So, with Cromwell as their leader, the Puritan part of the Church of England got the upper hand. They used their power with a considerable degree of moderation. All that Cromwell insisted upon was that every minister in the Church of England should be a godly man, and possess the gift of preaching; then he thought it did not signify whether they were Baptists, or Independents, or Episcopalians, or Presbyterians; so he let every man keep his living provided he was at all competent to preach. The upper hand was then with the Calvinistic party.

Men got dissatisfied with Cromwell. He was a great man, but he was like every other man who gets power; he used it, and men began to think they might as well have a king as Cromwell a Protector. So, when he died, they would not endure the feeble sway of his son Richard, and Charles the Second was brought back. He was brought back upon full condition that there should be perfect religious equality; but as soon as ever he had his turn, he gave the sway to the Episcopal party, and they used it,—used it without moderation, used it without judgment, used it without godliness, used it without common humanity, as a madman might use his freedom when he at last escaped from his chain. They at once began making their rules of uniformity, and two thousand godly men, as you know, were expelled from the Church of England at once by the Act of Uniformity on Bartholomew's Day, 1662.

Two of Wesley's ancestors went forth with this two thousand,—his grandfather and his great-grandfather. His great-grandfather, finding that he could not preach,—for, when they were turned out of the Church of England, they were not allowed to preach anywhere ;—finding that he could not teach a school, though he had great learning; finding that whatever he attempted to do, the Church tried to starve him, he became a physician, for he had studied medicine in his youth. He practised medicine for a livelihood, and was an exceedingly good and excellent man. The grandfather of Wesley was a great linguist, and a distinguished Oriental scholar. He also came out, and one reason why he was obliged to leave the Church was this, that he was required to be re-ordained. He said that he would not be re-ordained, for a thing could not have two beginnings : he believed he was an ordained minister of Jesus Christ, and God had given him seals to his ministry in the conversion of many souls, and he would not submit to be ordained again. Besides, he said, he considered the New Testament to be a sufficient rule of Christian worship without the Prayer Book ; he would not consent to anything added to it, and rejected the mere ceremonies of the Church.

This grandfather of Wesley had been in the habit of rambling about the country preaching the gospel everywhere, and the Church required him to stick to his own parish. He said he could not do it ; for God had called him to preach the Word wherever he had opportunity, and he would do it, and consequently he left the Church, though persuaded not to do so by many friends in it. He preached his farewell sermon in his little parish church from this text, "And now, brethren, I commend you to God, and to the word of His grace," and then went forth amidst the tears of his people, like Abraham, not knowing whither he went. He went into a town, but the magistrates of the town gave him orders to leave at once, they did not want him there.

There had been a law passed that no minister might go into a town in which he had preached, nor within five miles of any borough town, and he found it difficult to find an asylum anywhere. He was hunted about from place to place, and had some thoughts of going to America; but Providence, which had ordained that Wesley should be here, arranged that his grandfather should remain here. He began to preach privately among two or three friends, until his meetings, which were held in their own parlours, were attended by ten or a dozen people. He was frequently in prison, and constantly being fined. He had a large family, and had many stern trials in order to provide them even with bread. At last, when he died, that glorious Church refused sepulture to his body, because he had dared to preach the gospel after his own conscience, and his wife was constrained to take his corpse away from the church door, and put it in some hidden spot, where, without a stone, he lies, and no man can tell the place of his burial till the trump of the archangel shall sound, and he shall rise.

Samuel Wesley, the father of John Wesley, singularly enough grew up a Churchman. He was trained by his father; but early in life, when he began to judge for himself, he saw his father's poverty, and the way he had to wander about like those of old: I suppose that may have influenced his judgment, and he preferred some easier life. He became a Churchman, and, like most men who go from one extreme, he ran to the other, and became a very High Churchman. He was so high a Churchman that he got as his reward the little rectory of Epworth, where he was a preacher for forty years. I am sorry I cannot say he was a preacher of the gospel, but I am half afraid he was not; I hope he knew the gospel towards the close of his life. He was a very good man, a very excellent man as far as that went; but, I fear, he did not know the great truth of justification by faith in Christ. For very many years he preached very good moral sermons, visited the sick, and laid himself out with all his might to do all the good he possibly could, and he was so far a good man.

It is noteworthy that Samuel Wesley married the

daughter of Dr. Samuel Annesley, a noted Puritan divine, who had been expelled, and she became a Churchwoman; whether out of love to Samuel Wesley or not, I do not know; but she was not much of a Churchwoman, as I shall presently have to show you. She was a very orderly woman, one of the most orderly I have ever heard of. You know, in Scripture, the names of the mothers of the kings of Israel and Judah are often given,—"his mother's name was" so-and-so; because that is the key to any man's character. As to the father, it does not so much matter; but if you will tell us what a man's mother is, we can tell within a little what the man is.

Mr. Wesley's habits of order, perseverance, and determination, came to him as his mother's dowry. She had nineteen children, of whom nine died in infancy. As the income of the little rectory was only £130 a year, she must have had plenty of order, I think, in order to make £130 a year maintain herself, her husband, and so large a number of children. John Wesley was the twelfth of these children.

Having so many children, they could not afford to have a teacher in the house to instruct them, and the mother became the teacher, and an extraordinary teacher she was; for her habits of order began with the children almost from their birth. When they were three months old, we are told that she used to let them sleep three hours in the morning and three hours in the afternoon, and never more; they were put in the cradle, and rocked all that time whether they slept or not. The third three months they had to sleep two hours before dinner and two hours after. The last three months of the first year they had to sleep one hour before dinner and one hour after, never more, never less; and after that time, when they had attained the mature age of one year, they were never allowed to sleep at all except at night. When the night came on, they were put to bed at their regular hour exactly as the clock struck, and no cries or tears could prevail on her to allow them to stop up any longer. In the morning they got up at a certain time, and never a moment later.

Everything in the house was done after the same rule and method, and the Methodism of John Wesley, I have no doubt, came from the singular methodism of his mother, she arranging everything by method; her laws were as fixed as those of the Medes and Persians, which cannot by any means be altered.

When Mr. Wesley went out on any business, Mrs. Wesley used to conduct family prayer; she would take the Bible down, or read the prayers, or pray extemporarily. Her husband being on one occasion a long time from home, he had procured a curate to officiate for him. This curate was a man who, once upon a time, had had a bad debt, somebody had owed him sixpence, and had not paid him, and from that time he determined he would always preach about people paying their debts. Whatever the subject or whatever the sermon, he constantly insisted upon preaching upon paying your debts. It is said that Mr. Wesley, on one occasion, requested him to preach upon something else, and gave him this text—" Being justified by faith we have peace with God," and he said, " Faith, my dear friends, shows itself in the man who has it in a great many ways, among the rest, it always makes him pay his debts." The parishioners had been used to some little variety, though they had not heard very great gospel preaching, and complained a little.

One Sabbath evening, when Mrs. Wesley was reading her chapter to her children, she also read them a sermon. Two or three of the neighbours were there, and they said it was a better sermon than those read by the curate. The next Sunday evening, twenty or thirty neighbours came in, and Mrs. Wesley read a sermon to them. The next night there were so many there that the kitchen was quite full, and Mrs.

Wesley read a chapter, and a sermon, and prayed.   Her husband heard of it, and he wrote back to say she must not do anything of the kind ; there were three reasons why she must not do so : the first was, it looked very particular ; the next was, her sex—it was unfitting for a woman to do this ; the third was, the fear that great censure might come upon himself, and his own prospects might be injured.

Mrs. Wesley replied, that as for it looking particular, she did not think that mattered, for every good thing looked particular in the eyes of wicked people ; as for her sex, she begged him to remember, that if she was a woman, yet when he was away, she was the head of the household, and being the head of the household, she ought to remember and conduct family worship.   Then, as to the fear of censure upon himself, she was sure she would be the very last to do anything that might make good men censure him ; but as for the opinion of the bad, she hoped that he was a wiser man than to take any notice of them.

So Mr. Wesley did not write again till the curate wrote and said, "things were going on in the most shocking manner ; Mrs. Wesley had turned the parsonage house into a conventicle, and by such irregular proceedings the Church was in danger of great scandal."   Whereupon Mr. Wesley, the High Churchman, was greatly alarmed : those ugly words, "conventicle" and "irregular proceedings", quite shocked him, and he wrote back desiring her to desist.   To which the good wife replied that, if he only said he *desired* her to desist, she could not and would not ; but that if he would *command* her to desist, and would undertake to bear all the responsibility upon his own head in the day of judgment for the perishing of those souls for lack of knowledge, and if he would certify that to her under his own hand and seal, she would desist, but that as to merely saying he *desired* it, she would not do anything of the kind.   All things considered, Mr. Wesley thought it was high time for him to go home, and himself preach; the only way to put an end to the difficulty was to carry the burden himself.

I do not know whether Master John, who was the twelfth child, was at that time sleeping his three hours before dinner and his three hours after dinner. While he was yet a little one, the famous fire occurred which is pictured in that engraving so dear to most Wesleyan minds. The parsonage house caught light, and the mother and father escaped with most of the children, but to their horror it was found at last that John was left. The father fell down upon his knees; he was utterly bewildered; he found he could do nothing; he rushed into the fire, and came back thinking it impossible to save his child. Little Master John waked up, and thought it was daylight; but as he found it was hot, he thought he would go to the window, and there he stood calmly and quietly while the good man his father was praying to God to deliver his son. Some strong men came under the window, lifted another upon their shoulders, and Master John was saved from the flames; and the good old man rose up and said, " Now, blessed be God, let the house burn; I am rich, for all my children are saved;" and there he returned thanks to God in the midst of the frost and snow, for it was the depth of winter. From that time, his mother loved him with a double tenderness. She said that a child whom God had spared in so extraordinary a manner must be meant for some great work, and he was the object of her earnest and perpetual prayers.

You may also, I think, guess that she was somewhat of an Arminian in her theology, for otherwise John would not have been such a pronounced Arminian. I think he received that from his mother as well as his orderly habits. He was sent to Charterhouse School, where he received a good education. So good a lad was he thought to be, and that was all his father knew about religion—boys being good and orderly, well-behaved in church, not cracking nuts here, or playing, as some did—that his father allowed him "to take the sacrament" when he was but eight years of age.

When he advanced somewhat, he was sent to Oxford, and there he distinguished himself by his great power of logic. He was a good linguist, and a very masterly scholar, but he most of all excelled in logic. After a time, he obtained a fellowship. You know that that is a very high and important position in the University of Oxford: a man who can obtain a fellowship has certainly taken to himself " a good degree ", and shows very great powers of mind. At Oxford his early religious habits became more and more strengthened. He began to read the *De Imitatione Christi*, or, as the translation is called, *The Christian's Pattern*, of Thomas à Kempis, that book which is all but Protestant, written by a Romanist, and also Bishop Jeremy Taylor's *Rules of Holy Living and Dying*, and he was very deeply impressed by both of these works.

He thought that fasting and prayer, and doing good, visiting prisoners, distributing to the sick and to the poor, were the things which would save his soul, and with his best endeavours he sought to save himself. He was a leading member of a small knot of good young men in Oxford, who, in the midst of ribaldry and rebuke, would maintain what they thought to be the right. They were called, " Bible Bigots," " The Godly Club," " The Holy Club," and such like, by the ungodly men of the University, who used the very worst means they could to cast ridicule upon them. To this club Whitefield belonged, and, like the rest, he sought salvation by the works of the law, and not by the righteousness of Christ.

Some time after, though Mr. Wesley had a very comfortable provision from his fellowship, it entered into his heart to go and preach to the poor colonists and Indians of Georgia. The same desire had also taken possession of his brother Charles and their friend George Whitefield. John wrote to his mother about his going, and she replied that if she had twenty sons, it was the highest object of her ambition that they should preach the gospel to the heathen. He went to preach in the town of Savannah. There he did not preach the gospel, but the law; and the law he preached was such severe law that the people of Savannah would not put up with it. They did all they could to annoy him. James Edward Oglethorpe, the Governor, having respect for Mr. Wesley, thought that he would do something that might change his creed and make him less severe, something that would relax the austerity of his doctrines, and make him a little milder. So he looked out a young lady, a very attractive young person, with the very euphonious and poetic name of Sophia Christiana Hopkey, with the intention of making a match. Miss Hopkey made up her mind she would marry Mr. Wesley anyhow. She came to him first as an inquirer about the way of salvation; her inquiries were very long and pro-tracted. No doubt she asked a great many questions; perhaps some very knotty points were discussed. When she found that others arose which it was not quite so con-venient to discuss, she asked Mr. Wesley if he would mind instructing her in the French language. He was very kind; he did not mind; and I daresay they conjugated the verb "to love" several times without Mr. Wesley seeing at all what she was at. He went on teaching her the French language, till at last he was taken ill, and she thought that in return for his great kindness, the least she could do would be to watch over him and nurse him. So there was this blessed angel always intent upon alleviating his bodily sufferings.

Mr. Wesley recovered, but found that he had got into a peculiar condition. His views about these matters were such that he could not do anything unless he had made it a matter of prayer; and as he was more than half a Moravian at that time, he went to a Moravian Bishop to ask his advice upon the subject. The Moravian Bishop said he would not give him advice unless he would promise to abide by it. The promise was given, and Wesley began his story:—" I suppose you know Miss Hopkey." I daresay you can guess quite as well as I can how he told his tale. The Bishop said he would let him know in a few days what the Lord's will was concerning her. When Wesley went to learn his decision, the Bishop said, "You must not marry her," whereupon Wesley replied, "The will of the Lord be done!" He had never made Miss Hopkey a promise of any kind, though there is little doubt she tried very hard indeed to induce him to do so. Soon after, she married a wealthy gentleman, named Williamson.

After her marriage, Mrs. Williamson did not think so much of Mr. Wesley ; she did not come regularly to attend his ministry, so the next time the communion came round, she was coming up, and he said, " No, I have one law for all ; you are not a regular attendant, and you cannot commune." Her friends came and expostulated ; but he said, " I feel that I am in an awkward position ; for some will say I do this out of spite, but God knows I have none whatever in my heart; I only treat her honestly and justly, as she should be treated, and she cannot commune."

The subject was taken up, and he was prosecuted for slandering her character, and refusing her church privileges; but though they tried very hard to pack the jury, and, I think, got forty-four jurymen instead of fifteen, yet he came out of it quite clear, and there was not a stain left upon his character. Still, he did no good whatever, and when he returned to England his ministry had been Christless and fruitless.

He had preached morality ; he had preached against drunkenness ; but no drunkards had become sober ; he had preached with all his might about leading a religious life and being much in prayer, but nobody had prayed the more ; he had earnestly exhorted men to flee from the wrath to come, but he had not told them where to flee to. He had done no good. In his own estimation his ministry was a perfect failure, and he came back and said, " I went to Savannah to convert the Indians, and I came back and found that I was not converted myself." For my part, I think his voyage was not fruitless if he only discovered that, and his trials were not in vain if they only brought him to seek his own salvation.

Upon his return to England, he used to meet with a few godly people who came together to read the Bible and religious books : such classes are perfectly allowable in the Church of England to this day. One night Wesley met with them, and " it seems," says one of his biographers, " that the evening was spent in reading *Luther on the Epistle to the Galatians,*"—elsewhere, the same writer says it was "when one was reading *Luther's Preface to the Epistle to the Romans*— that the light of gospel truth streamed in upon Mr. Wesley's eyes :" he found that by faith we stand accepted before God, and not by any feelings, doings, or righteousness of our own. Now that Wesley was really a converted man, he wanted to tell to everyone else what he had found out concerning the cross of Christ. But he did not feel himself fully qualified to do so till he had received more instruction, and therefore he took a journey, in order to visit the celebrated Moravian colonies at Marienborn and Herrnhut, under the command of Count Zinzendorf, that he might see how godly men lived.

He took his journey to Amsterdam, and, passing through Holland, was greatly pleased with its straight lines of canals, and trees all cut in one shape. Rocks piled in confusion, and rivulets rolling down their sides in cascades would not please him, but these straight rows did. He gained in-struction there, some good and some bad, and came back, as I think, with confused views, but yet knowing the essential and vital points of the gospel—that men are saved by the righteousness of Christ, and not by the deeds of the law.

The Church of England was at this time in a most deplorable state; some clergymen could not read, and if they could read, they had to stop to spell the hard words while they were reading the Prayer Book. Others of them had learning, but were the most debauched of characters; they were most at their ease on horseback following the hounds, and a great deal more lusty when they were roaring "The Roast Beef of Old England" at the farmer's table, than when they were pretending to preach the gospel of Christ. Nothing could be worse than the Church of England at that day. As for the Dissenters, they had been so long persecuted, that when the fires of martyrdom were quenched, they just lay comfortably down in their beds, and went to sleep. As Dr. Campbell told you, the Church was asleep in the dark, and the Dissenters were asleep in the light.

Wesley first commenced his work by expounding to different classes in the year 1738; he thought his work was to teach them the Word of God as he knew it. But Mr. Whitefield, who always led the way in everything, had preached out of doors at Islington, and afterwards at Kingswood, and Mr. Wesley coming down there, thought he would do the same. Mr. Whitefield introduced him to the congregation, and told them to listen to him. Great crowds came to listen to him, just as they had to the mighty seraph George. There he preached with great power, and there were manifestations attending his ministry of the same kind as those which have lately happened in the revivals in the North of Ireland. Men were smitten down, men and women screamed out in the midst of the preaching, the Spirit of God moved the heart in so terrible a manner, that even the flesh suffered in sympathy with it, and the very bones seemed to quiver while the sword of God went through the hearts of the people. They were made to feel that it was an awful thing to stand in the presence of an angry God.

Whitefield, while preaching at Kingswood among the poor colliers, whose tears had made white gutters down their black sooty cheeks, determined that he would have a school in which to teach the children of the colliers. As he could not get a piece of ground on which to erect a building, he took a large stone, laid it down, and said, "I have laid the first stone of this school in this place, and if it has to be erected elsewhere, move the stone; let that be the first stone, and I commend (said he) the enterprise to my dear brother, Mr. John Wesley, let him carry it out while I am gone to America." Wesley did so; he built the school, and though I think it was Whitefield's property, for he found and collected most of the money, Wesley managed, when the quarrel arose between them, to get that on his own account. I cannot quite see how he did it, I must leave that to his defenders to clear up; it is a little point on which I have some question.

When Mr. Whitefield came back, he preached in Moorfields, a place where all the ruffians of London went out to play, and where puppet-shows, and amusements of that description, were carried on. Whitefield having preached there, John Wesley would do the same; he also preached on Kennington Common to always increasing crowds.

Whitefield and Wesley agreed that all doctrinal points should be left, that they would only preach a full Christ to perishing sinners, and that they should only take as the sum and substance of their preaching, justification by faith and the regenerating work of the Holy Spirit. They thus made a sort of compromise, but no such compromise can ever last, and this did not. As soon as either of them began to think, he found that they could not get on well together.

In Moorfields was a place called the Foundry, which had been used by the Government for casting cannon, but for more than twenty years had been in ruins. By a terrible explosion, attended with fatal consequences to several of the workmen, and serious injuries to others, while recasting cannon taken from the French, the place was almost wrecked, and then abandoned. Mr. Wesley was urged by some friends to preach in it, which he did, and after a while it was purchased and put in repair, and became the first Methodist meeting-house in London.

In this Methodist Society there were many Calvinists as well as Arminians; I suppose the larger proportion held Calvinistic sentiments. Among them was one good man named Acourt, who came to John Wesley, and complained that Charles had stopped his quarterly ticket because he held the doctrine of predestination. "Well," said Wesley, "Charles cannot keep you away for that, because we leave all that alone; we agreed to do that, and I suppose you do not talk much about it." "Oh, yes, I do!" said the old man, "it is the joy of my heart." "But," said Wesley, "you need not talk about it in our Society." "Yes," he said, "I always do so whenever I can; I mean to try to convert all my friends, and agitate the matter as much as I can." Wesley said, "But you know the Society is founded on mutual agreement that this question shall not be entertained." "But I must speak; I believe it to be such a vital point that I mean to agitate it as much as ever I can." "Well," said Wesley, "I do not see what I am to do with you; if I turn you out, there will be a great many others likeminded."

He found out that this compromise could not go on, for, at the same time, John Cennick, who had been put into the schoolroom at Kingswood, which had been built by Whitefield and Wesley conjointly, had become an out and out Calvinist, and began preaching the gospel in the fulness of it. Wesley, hearing of it, came down and said, "This won't do, you must not preach like this, you must give it up." "Well," said the man, "I have not altered, I always preached like this." "No," said Wesley, "I hardly think you did." "Yes," said he, "I always did, and now the point begins to be raised, I cannot alter it, and I believe you are in the wrong." "Then," said Wesley, "I must turn you out; and it has come to this, that those who are of one opinion must go one way, and those who are of another opinion must go the other." And so Mr. Cennick and about half the members left, and there was a Tabernacle built where Whitefield preached, and half the members remained as followers of Mr. Wesley.

Then there came the great division between Whitefield and Wesley : never were they divided in heart, though they were divided in other respects. I do not believe in compromises myself; I have not a pinch of that kind of thing in my nature. Union chapels always lead to "the union", in my opinion, and these compromises between truth and error always lead, in the end, to error becoming triumphant. These two men of God were much better apart, to go forth and preach their own views as they believed them, without quarrelling; for I am sure that if they had attempted to remain together they must have quarrelled. When Mr. Whitefield came back, Wesley said to him, "You preach your views and I will preach mine, and," he said, "you can preach in the Foundry if you like." Whitefield took him at his word, and preached such a sermon upon the decrees of God and predestination, that Wesley said, "We cannot have this any more." They separated, and I do verily believe there was twice as much good done as there could have been had they constantly acted together.

Well, after a time George Whitefield died, having finished his work, and Wesley remained far longer upon earth ; in fact, he remained to an extreme old age, still to be the head of his Society. But in the year 1770, John Wesley did that which I cannot sufficiently condemn. He found the members of his company, as he said, were leaning too much towards Calvinism. Even though he had turned out all the Calvinists, and they had separated, yet again that very wicked system, Calvinism, would spring up,—there is such vitality and life in it that it will be constantly rising,— and Mr. Wesley, in order to cure the leaning of his ministers towards this, passed certain "minutes" at the Conference, which, as I read them, I am sure will shock your mind. In the book which I have here they are defended, the book being written by one of Wesley's ardent admirers in America ;* but if they do not teach that which is quite contrary to the gospel, I think they do not teach anything at all.

I ought to say that, in the next year, Mr. Wesley made an apology for them, and said that he never did mean to teach anything but justification by faith ; but in his ardour to put down Calvinism in the ranks of his own people, he ran not only away from Calvinism, but away from Jesus Christ and His truth altogether.

Mr. Tyerman† says, " As Wesley's Theological Theses led to the longest and bitterest controversy in his history, we subjoin them in their entirety "—

" ' We said, in 1744, we have leaned too much toward Calvinism. Wherein ?

" I. With regard to man's faithfulness.

" Our Lord Himself taught us to use the expression ; and we ought never to be ashamed of it. We ought steadily to assert, on His authority, that, if a man is not ' faithful in the unrighteous mammon', God will not give him the true riches.

---

* The title of the book is, "*Wesley and his Coadjutors.* By Rev. William C. Larrabee, A.M. Edited by Rev. B. F. Tefft, D.D. [2 vols. cr. 8vo.] Cincinnati : 1851."

† Wesley's doctrinal theses as read by Mr. Spurgeon are not reported. We have therefore supplied the omission from the *Rev. L. Tyerman's "Life and Times of Wesley."* Vol. III., pp. 72-3.

" II. With regard to working for life.

" This also our Lord has expressly commanded us: Labour εργαζεσθε, literally, ' Work for the meat that endureth to everlasting life.' And, in fact, every believer, till he comes to glory, works for as well as from life.

" III. We have received it as a maxim, that ' a man is to do nothing in order to justification.' Nothing can be more false. Whoever desires to find favour with God should ' cease from evil, and learn to do well.'

"Whoever repents, should do ' works meet for repentance.' And if this is not in order to find favour, what does he do them for?

" Review the whole affair.

" 1. Who of us is now accepted of God? He that now believes in Christ with a loving and obedient heart.

" 2. But who among those that never heard of Christ? He that feareth God and worketh righteousness, according to the light he has.

" 3. Is this the same with ' he that is sincere'? Nearly, if not quite.

" 4. Is not this ' salvation by works'? Not by the merit of works, but by works as a condition.

" 5. What have we been disputing about for these thirty years? I am afraid, about words.

" 6. As to merit itself, of which we have been so dreadfully afraid; we are rewarded ' according to our works,' yea, ' because of our works.' How does this differ from, ' for the sake of our works'? And how differs this from secundum merita operum? as our works deserve? Can you split this hair? I doubt I cannot.

" 7. The grand objection to one of the preceding propositions is drawn from matter of fact. God does in fact justify those who, by their own confession, neither feared God nor wrought righteousness. Is this an exception to the general rule? It is a doubt, God makes any exception at all. But how are we sure, that the person in question never did fear God and work righteousness? His own saying so is not proof; for we know how all that are convinced of sin undervalue themselves in every respect.

" 8. Does not talking of a justified or a sanctified state tend to mislead men? almost naturally leading them to trust in what was done in one moment?

"Whereas we are every hour and every moment pleasing or displeasing to God, ' according to our works'; according to the whole of our inward tempers, and our outward behaviour."

This seems to me to be as plain a description of salvation by works as could possibly have been given. Well, this led to a tremendous conflict. Whitefield had just died, but he left some successors. First came Sir Richard Hill, who assailed Mr. Wesley furiously. Then followed Rowland Hill, who, with all manner of wit, pounced down upon Wesley, using some very strong and unjustifiable language. Next came John Macgowan, and he, without any coarseness, but with sparkling wit, attacked the Wesleys and Mr. Fletcher.

Then arose the champion of the controversy, Mr. Toplady, and he, with great force, but with extraordinary bitterness, assailed them both with all his might, calling Mr. Wesley "The Old Fox tarred and feathered," and such like expressions. Mr. Hervey, by the way, had also come in at an early period, and certain letters which he had written against Mr. Wesley had been printed after his death, and had done very great damage to John's cause, so he had a pretty considerable number of opponents. The Wesleyans say that all the bitterness was on the Calvinists' side. Now, I do not think it is well to use bad names in controversy; calling the man "an old fox" did not do any good, they could just as well prove he was mistaken, without calling him by opprobrious names.

But, to say the truth, Mr. Fletcher, of Madeley, who took Wesley's side of the question, was the worst controversialist of the lot, a great deal the worst; for, without using bad names, he, in the most quiet and pious manner, blasphemes. I do not know whether you understand what I mean, but you know there are different ways of a man's cursing another. One does it in "Billingsgate", but that is very low and common. Another one does it genteelly. Fletcher could write against attributes which are high and glorious, and yet write of them as if he meant to defend those very attributes, and would vindicate God. And Thomas Coke and Mr. Wesley certainly used some very shocking and opprobrious titles themselves;

they were, I think, quite as bad as the others as to the manifestation of bitterness.

As to the point in question, it is hard to say which did conquer. In a controversy, you know, sometimes the worst side gets the best of it, and a controversy is no test of truth; but I think that the Calvinists must have overcome if they could have seen the way to fight. As it was, they fought about decrees. Those on the Calvinistic side should have said, "We will begin with facts. Now, Mr. Wesley, is it not a fact that many are saved, and many are lost?" No one could deny but that there are some who are saved and some who are lost. "Who saves those that are saved?" "God does it." "Very good: then, if God does it, He always purposed to do it." It is a very easy step from that, and Calvinism is proved at once beyond all chance of refutation; but while you always keep on fighting as to the decrees, you are at a disadvantage. Had they but come to close quarters upon matters of fact, I think we know which would have won the victory.

The controversy was exceedingly bitter on both sides, and Mr. Wesley did not distinguish himself by his fairness. He misrepresented our views; he put words into the lips of Mr. Toplady, for instance, that he never uttered, and, at the last,—and this was a piece of cruelty which is to be pardoned, since he is in heaven, and God has pardoned him,—he announced from the pulpit that Mr. Toplady, on his dying bed, had renounced the doctrines which he had preached, and that he died in terror and in fear. All this was totally false, and witnesses, who had marked the triumphant entrance of Mr. Toplady into his glorious rest, were willing to prove that it was an utterly unfounded slander. I do not think Wesley was the inventor of it, but it is ill to propagate a falsehood such as this; but let any one of us who is without fault, who has never told a tale against his neighbour, come and throw the first stone.

The Methodists thought it was their duty to dismiss Mr. Fletcher from the Presidency of Trevecca College, and also from the Tutorship. They said they could never have any dealings with those who had so undermined the truth as it is in Christ; but next year Mr. Wesley and his brother signed a document to the effect that what he had said was, perhaps, incorrect, and that he had not meant to teach anything but justification by faith. But he did as good as retrace his steps, for he got Mr. Fletcher to write in vindication of the mistake he had made, thereby undoing his confession; confessing that he was wrong, and getting another to prove that he was right. I know not how to speak of such strange dealing—I should not like to use the word " shuffling "— but I think that I may call it double-dealing.

Let us now leave these controverted doctrinal points, and see what Wesley was doing and suffering for the cause which he had espoused. He went down to his father's village of Epworth, and he thought that as the rector had obtained the living entirely through his father, the least thing he could do would be to let the son preach in the church. But no, the church was closed against him, he could not be allowed to enter; so, going to the churchyard, he picked out his father's tomb, and there he stood and preached the Word of God. God was present there, and one or two were smitten down. He stayed a week, and preached constantly upon his father's tomb; a great revival followed. He preached with great faithfulness. If he recognized an individual in the crowd, he would seek him out and ask him, " Are you a believer in Christ? Do you know the regenerating influence of the Holy Spirit?" and so forth; and there were very many who could call him their spiritual father.

At this place, a number of his followers—a waggon-load of Methodists—were apprehended, and taken before the magistrates. When they were brought up, one magistrate asked what their crime was, and some one said, "They make people get up at 4 o'clock in the morning, and they are always praying; and, besides that, they have converted my wife." "Well," the magistrate said, "what have they done to her?" "Well," said he, "before she was converted, she was the biggest scold in the parish; but ever since she has been a convert she has been quite a quiet soul; I never saw such a difference." The magistrate said to the Wesleyans, "Go home, my good people; convert all the scolds in the parish. I am sure if you never do anything worse than that, you had better go your own way." But they did not always meet with such a good reception as this. From among the converts, several young preachers, laymen, as they are called, had risen up in Wesley's connexion, and Wesley at first tried to put a stop to their preaching, as it was "irregular " but his mother said she had heard Thomas Maxfield preach, "and," said she, "John, you cannot stop him; it is God's work, he must preach;" and he did. Some of these young preachers went about to different places, among others to Wednesbury, and many there became Methodists.

At this time there was great national excitement on account of the Pretender. The enemies of Mr. Wesley stated that he was disloyal to the reigning house, and wanted to put an end altogether to the Protestant succession, and so forth. It was reported that the Pretender travelled about with John Wesley in disguise; so the mob, led by the nose, attacked the houses of Methodists in Wednesbury, entered many, and broke their furniture. John heard of it, and said, "I shall go and preach there." So he rode on horseback into Wednesbury, and at noon, in the middle of the town, preached to a congregation far greater than he ever expected, and was not molested. But several hours afterwards, when he was quietly writing in the house of one of the members of the Society, an immense mob gathered round the house. I will read you some account of their proceedings, because it will be a specimen of what very frequently occurred to Mr. Wesley in his journeys :—

"Toward night the mob surrounded the house, roaring, 'Bring out Wesley.' Wesley sent for the leader to come in. He came. Wesley took him by the hand, spoke a word or two, when the lion became a lamb. Wesley then told him to go out and bring in two or three of the most angry of the company. He went, and returned with two, who were so furious, they were ready to 'swallow the ground with rage.' In two minutes they became as calm as their captain. Wesley then went boldly out into the crowd, stood up on a chair, and began to address them. After a while he asked them, 'What would ye have me do?' 'We want you to go with us to the magistrate.' 'I will go cheerfully; shall we go now?' 'Yes, now.' 'Well, come on,' said Wesley, and walked along followed by several hundreds. The residence of the magistrate was two miles distant. Night came on, with a heavy rain. Well, the magistrate would not listen to them, but told them to 'go home and be quiet.' But no; to a magistrate they would have him go, so it was proposed by one of the mob that they should take him to another magistrate, at Walsall. On, therefore, through rain and mud they tramped, only to find that the magistrate had gone to bed; so they concluded to scatter home, about fifty accompanying Mr. Wesley to protect him. These fifty were his friends, who had mingled with the mob, in order to aid him when necessary.

"They had not proceeded a hundred yards, when the Walsall mob came pouring in like a flood, bearing all before them. His friends stood for a while stoutly in his defence; but they were vastly outnumbered. After being many times knocked down, all but four ran away, and left him. These four stood fast. One of them was a woman. She knocked down, outright, four Walsall men, one after another, and would have whipped the whole mob, laying them all sprawling at her feet, had not four men seized her at once, and held her, while a fifth pounded away on her, till they were ashamed to be seen—five men fighting one woman—and then they let her go. Being deprived of his valiant defender, he was borne along by the multitude. It was dark, slippery, and down hill. They tried to trip him up, and get him down, that he might be trampled to death; but he was too spry for them, and kept on his feet. They struck at him; but as he was low of stature, and it was dark, they struck over him, and knocked their own friends down. They seized hold of his clothes; but they could not seem to hold him, as their hands would either slip their hold, or the garment would give way. They kept crying out, 'Knock his brains out;' 'Hang him;' 'Drown him;' 'Kill the dog outright;' 'Throw him into the river;' 'Away with him;' and some even exclaimed, '*Crucify him, crucify him!*' During all this time, Wesley was as calm as if he had been sitting in his study. It only came into his mind once, he says, that if they should throw him into the river, it *might spoil the papers in his pocket.*"

Now which of us would have been as calm as that? He would frequently get into such a mess as that, but was always as calm and cool.

On one occasion, at Falmouth, when he found that there was a mob around the house, in which he was visiting a lady who was sick, he sat in a room with nothing but a thin partition between him and the mob in the passage. All in the house had escaped except Wesley, the invalid, and a servant girl. A lot of privateer sailors began to push away at the partition. As the partition was falling, he quietly removed a looking-glass which hung on it, to prevent its being broken. When the privateers came in, he said to them, "Have I done you any hurt?" They said, "No, sir, no, you have not done us any hurt." "Well," said he, "who wants me; whom have I hurt ? " Then he said to one of them, " I think very likely you would like to hear me preach." They said they would not have any objection. So they fetched out a chair for him, and the privateers stood around, and said, " Let us hear the fellow preach." So he began, and kept on as short a time as he well could, thinking it best not to trust too long to their leniency. He says he always found that the only way to deal with a mob was to look at them right straight in the face. If he had flinched for a moment, he might very soon have had his life taken away. He learned to look them straight in the face : they feared him when he did not fear them.

After wishing these Falmouth rioters " good night," he got out of the crowd, mounted his horse, and rode away to a village at some little distance, where he had to preach that night. When he reached the top of the hill, some good people came running to him, and said, " Mr. Wesley ! Mr. Wesley ! " " What is the matter ? " he asked. " Turn back again," they replied. " Why ? " said he. They then told him that the minister, hearing he was coming, had procured a writ, and the constables were watching for him. " Then," said he, " I will go and see what it is all about," and he rode till he met the people. " What are you looking for ? " They replied, " We are looking for John Wesley." " Well," said he, " I am the very individual ; what do you want with me ? " The constable did not know what to say, but at last said, " I have been told, Mr. Wesley, as they say that you have got the Pretender with you." He answered, " I cannot think that the gentlemen are so foolish as to believe anything of the kind, it is too foolish and absurd, and as you have nothing to say to me I will go on," and so he went on to preach.

On another occasion the constables came in too late, he had just finished his sermon ; they said, " You must not preach in this town." " I don't want to do so," was his reply, " I have just done."

At this time they began to worry his preachers, and they adopted this singular way, and a most frightful way it was. The press-gang system prevailed, by which men were forced, not only into the navy, but into the army ; and the law was, that any man who was a vagabond, and had no certain means of subsistence, could be forced into the army. Now, Mr. Wesley's preachers, not being ordained by the Church of England, came, as their enemies liked to construe the Act, under the title of vagabonds, having no sufficient means of subsistence.

The first they took was John Nelson, a mason, an extraordinary man, who had been converted under Mr. Wesley. The press-gang seized John Nelson, and took him for a soldier. He said he could not be a soldier, he was enlisted already in another service, in the service of the Lord Jesus Christ, and he could not and would not be a soldier. They insisted that he should, and as he would not take the enlistment money, he was cast into prison, a prison so filthy that not even a dog should have been put there. Before he was put in, "the magistrates delivered him over to the captain, who read to him the articles of war, adding, 'You see your doom is death, if you disobey us.' 'I do not fear the man that can kill me, any more than I fear the man that can cut down a dog-weed,'" said John.

They marched him off to Bradford, and threw him into a dungeon immediately under a slaughter-house, the bottom filled with blood and filth in a dreadful state of putrefaction. The hardest heart was softened at his sufferings. One man in the town, who had been his enemy, offered the captain £10 to let him give Nelson a bed for the night. Another poor soldier said he would be bail for him ; but the captain said he would dash his brains out if he did not mind what he was after. His captors gave him no food, but early in the morning the good people of the town came and brought him something to eat.

He was marched from thence, under a guard, to Leeds. The other pressed men were ordered to the ale-house, but he was sent to prison! People came in crowds, and looked at him through the iron grating. Some said it was a shame to treat a Methodist so ; others said it served him right, and they wished the Methodists were all hanged. "We cannot," they said, "get drunk or swear, but what some Methodist fellow comes and tells us of it."

Nelson was next marched to York, and taken before some officers whom he reproved for swearing. The officers told him he must not preach to them, and he said, "There is only one way of stopping my preaching. You swear ; and if it is right to swear, it must be right to preach ; you stop swearing, and I will stop telling you of it." As he was marched through York, he himself said it seemed as if hell was moved at his coming ; they took him through the town as if he had been some great champion taken in battle. He was put in jail with the very worst of sinners, but he began preaching to them, and many were converted.

He was sent out to drill along with the corporal, but he began to tell him the way of salvation, and the corporal forgot all about "Shoulder arms !" Seeing this, they sent him out to drill in company with a number of others, but instead of marching with them, he began to tell them the right way to heaven. The citizens came to listen to him, and there were generally large congregations just at the time the men ought to have been drilling. This was very inconvenient indeed ; it was felt that it would put an end to all discipline ; and as the people of the town began to sympathize with him, he was marched off somewhere else. An officer, with a horrible oath, said to him, "Sir, you have been preach-ing." "I have," was the reply. "I will have no preaching or praying in this regiment." "Then you must have no swearing, for I have as much right to preach as you have to swear." "Then you shall be flogged, if you preach," said the officer. " Something worse than flogging will happen to you if you do not leave off swearing." The officer, in a towering passion, said, " Corporal, take this man to prison." As he was being conducted there, a superior officer met him, and said, " John Nelson, what are you going to be put in prison for?" "For preaching." " For preaching? is that all? I shall come and hear you myself: that is no crime. I wish all men were like you; go back to your quarters."

Nelson was a very strict teetotaler. After he had done his sermon one day, an alderman of the town said to him, " Nelson, come in and have something to drink." " No," said Nelson, " I do not mind going home with you, but I cannot drink any liquor," and he did not. On one of these occasions, an officer came to him on Sunday evening, and said, " You have not been to church to-day." " Yes, I have," said he, " and if you had been there, you would have seen me." The officer said, " I will have none of your impudence. I suppose you have been preaching." " Not yet, but I mean to." " If you do," said the officer, " I will punish you severely." This petty tyrant ordered one of the soldiers to put a cockade in Nelson's hat, and swore he should wear it. This, Nelson said, made him feel a bone of the old man stir within him, for he felt that he could easily tie the little fellow's head and heels together, and pitch him over the fence; but it would have brought reproach on the gospel, and so he would not do it.

John Wesley came to see him, and said to him, " You can preach better than I can; you can travel free of expense, and who can tell what good you may do?" They were obliged to let this very ugly customer go; for the Countess of Huntingdon made an appeal to the Crown, and he was set free.

Others did not come off so well. Thomas Beard, a

quiet and peaceable man, was torn from his wife and children, and sent away because he preached ; he fell sick with a fever, and died. John Downes was taken up by the press-gang, carried off, and he died in the service. Another of Wesley's preachers was arrested, but he was let go. Thomas Maxfield was impressed, and kept for a long time.

Among the rest, they arrested a Methodist clergyman, a Mr. Meriton, of the Isle of Wight. When he was taken before the magistrates, he said, " I suppose you do not know what you are doing ; I am a regular clergyman of the Church of England. There are my orders. I have been ordained by the Bishop, and it is a strange thing that a clergyman cannot go through the streets without being arrested by a press-gang." The magistrates were in trepidation, and so were the press-gang. He said, "Gentlemen, I will forgive you if you will sit still, and let me preach a sermon to you." So the justices and all the others had to hear a thoroughly evangelical sermon, and, I dare say, for once they received a little knowledge of the gospel as well as the law.

One rascal declared he would impress John Wesley himself ; so when Wesley was preaching with a crowd around him, he cried out, " Arrest that man, take him, I arrest him in the name of the king, I will take him into his service." Wesley said, " Do you want me ? I will come with you in a moment." Mr. Wesley said to him, as soon as he had talked himself fairly dry and out of breath, "I suppose you know I am a clergyman of the Church of England, regularly ordained, and you are liable to prosecution and very severe punishment for what you have done ? " " What do you mean, sir ? " " For arresting me and taking me into His Majesty's service." " *I* arrest you, my dear sir ! I did not think of such a thing ; I merely asked you home to dinner, and you said you would come, but (says he) if it is at all unpleasant to you, sir, I should not at all wish to detain you. Perhaps you would like to go back, sir?" So John said he thought he rather should, and the officer in this way got out of the scrape. He said, "I will go back with you, sir, if you like; perhaps there are some people there who may annoy you." So he rode back with Mr. Wesley, and took him to the place with the greatest possible politeness. He found he had caught a Tartar, and had made a great mistake in arresting the wrong man. The great coolness of Wesley would always enable him, when he had got into any of these difficulties, to get out a great deal sooner than the most of men.

We must say something about the Wesleys as preachers. Mr. Wesley preached a great number of times. Dr. Campbell told us last Friday night that Mr. Whitefield delivered 78,000 sermons. I put my finger to my head and thought, Dear me, however could he have done it? I went home, and, consulting a book, I found it was 18,000 sermons. I was certain that no being who ever lived could have preached 78,000 sermons; for he would have had to preach at the rate of 1,000 a year; that would be nearly 20 a week, and have to be kept up for 78 years, which nobody could do. Wesley, however, preached oftener than Whitefield, for his life was very much longer. Besides that, he established schools for his Society, and organized the present Bible Society of the Wesleyan Methodists.

At the first Conference, there were only six ministers, at the next, eleven; but they have increased till, I think, now there are some thousands of ministers and lay preachers connected with them, and I cannot tell how many members, possibly 200,000 or 300,000; the number is immense. They are still managed very much on the same system as that which Mr. Wesley invented.

Besides all this, he published 55 volumes of literature—biographies and so forth; there was very little for his people to read, and he published a library for them. In fact, his system touched upon everything—told them what time to get up in the morning and what time to go to bed; it not only touched on religion, but other matters besides. He wrote grammars of the French, English, Latin, and Greek languages, and very respectable grammars, too, which he wished to be used by all Methodist young men. He did his reading on horseback, as he rode along to fulfil his different engagements, and so read the whole range of literature. He was a great reader, and seems to have had a most capacious mind.

He had a wife—no, he had no *wife*, he was married to a lady whom we could not venture to call a wife, it would be degrading the name. It was unfortunate for Mr. Wesley that he had this wife at all, and I cannot make out how it came to pass. There was a Mrs. Murray, a very excellent woman, who had been early left a widow, and was chosen by Mr. Wesley to take the charge of the Home which he had at Newcastle; for Wesley was in the habit of picking up poor men and women and orphan children, and providing for them. He gave Mrs. Murray charge over this Home, and she proved to be so good and gracious a woman, that he wished her to go to the other Homes,—to be, in fact, a sort of matron of them all, to take the oversight of the Society. At last he thought it was God's will that he should be married to Mrs. Murray, and it was arranged. They seemed to have been precisely the two persons who should have been married; it was agreed upon, and they were to be married in October. To Mr. Wesley's consternation,—and this is an extraordinary circumstance, the bottom of which has never been reached,—he received news from Mr. Whitefield and his brother Charles, that Mrs. Murray had, the day before, married Mr. John Bennett, one of the Wesleyan preachers. He took the news in his usual calm way, and nobody thought that he felt it at the time; but he did feel it acutely. It is said that it was managed by Charles and Mr. Whitefield, on the ground that they thought he would not be so useful if he were married, and they therefore got this Mr. Bennett to marry her, so that brother John might be kept out of the snare of the fowler. Others say Mr. Whitefield had no hand in it, and lay the blame on Charles, but I cannot understand how it could have been at all; it is a most singular thing. Mr. Wesley saw the couple a few days afterwards; it was a very bitter trial to him, and one which he never forgot, for he seems always to have remembered her: it appears to me to have been one of the most extraordinary things that could have happened to any man.

I do not know how he felt, for it was such a strange affair; but he afterwards married that sweet-tempered lady who so ill-treated him throughout his married life. A contract was made between them before marriage, that he should not travel a mile less, nor preach a sermon less on that account, and to that she agreed; but she soon found that she could not endure it; and, not content with quarrelling because he was often away, she began to indulge in the most foolish jealousies, and to hate him with a thorough hatred. Any letters which he wrote to the young people of the congregation she would try to intercept, and when she had got a letter written to any of the females of the congregation, she would interpolate words of her own of the very basest kind, and show them everywhere, and even went the length of printing them in the newspapers in order to injure him. She would go away from home, and then he would beg her to come back, when she would behave worse than before. When she went away the last time, he said, he did not forsake her, and he did not dismiss her, but he would not recall her.

On one occasion he had promised to take Mr. Charles Wesley's daughter to Canterbury for a ride. Charles said

to him, "Your wife has a lot of letters which she has shown
to me, and they are to be published in the *Morning Post*
to-morrow; you must stop at home and prevent that."
John said : "No, Charles; when I gave myself up to
serve the Lord, I never made any reserve as to my purse,
my person, my time, my talents, or my reputation, but
surrendered them all to God. I shall not remain here one
moment to defend myself. Tell Sarah I shall take her to
Canterbury to-morrow. The child shall not be disappointed
by me." That was gloriously well said.

I think Mr. Wesley had a dash of wit in him. Two or
three fanatics came to see him one day, and they said, "You
are not born again ; the thing is very easily done, and we
are going to stop this morning, and regenerate you before
we go." He said, "If you want to wait, you may wait;
I will just show you in ; this way." He took them to the
door of the chapel,—a large, cold chapel it was in
the winter, and having got them in, he shut the door
on them. He kept them there till their courage was
cooled ; but the promised operation was not performed.

Sometimes his enemies would try to get some of his
church-members, and make them drunk, to ruin them. They
got one into a public-house and made him thoroughly
drunk, and then they stood him up, and said, "There is
a Methodist !" That sobered him in a moment. He
knocked them all down, took the landlord and put him on
the hob, broke all the bottles, locked the door, and walked
home, for which I really commend him. Whatever damage
he may have done, I think was very richly deserved, and
the landlord perhaps was in a very proper place.

When Wesley was aged eighty-six years, he went down
to Falmouth,—to that Falmouth where the privateers had
besieged the house, and broken down the partition, —and when
he went there, there were thousands in the streets coming to
meet him, women waving their handkerchiefs in the balconies,

men standing with their hats off, and he rode along like some great conqueror in triumph. All this happened in the place where, in his earlier days, he had been despised and rejected of men. Now there was no one who had so many hearers and lovers as the venerable old man; and in the same town hundreds of children would run after him, and Wesley, with his locks flowing down his back, put his hand upon their heads, and blessed them in the name of God. It seemed to be something like the entrance of Christ into the City of Jerusalem, and the children crying "Hosanna."

He lived to be almost idolized by his followers, and common opinion turned completely round. Those who had opposed him the most, bitterly regretted that they had done so. Rowland Hill said he had spent the first part of his life in fighting the white devil, Arminianism, but he meant to spend the rest of his life in fighting the black devil, Antinomianism; and Mr. Berridge, when he saw him, said, "What fools we have been; we ought to have been turning the world upside down while we have been quarrelling with one another." At eighty-eight Wesley entered into his rest, and it could be said of him that, when his debts were paid, he had not £10 in the world. When they wanted to know how he would dispose of his plate, he said he had two silver spoons, one in London and one in York, and that there were so many poor people about that he had not got any more.

Peace to his ashes, death to his errors, life to all the truth he preached, and may the blessing of God make any one of us but a tenth as earnest as he was, and a tenth as useful! With what we think to be clearer views of Divine truth, we can only justify our belief by being more zealous and more devoted to the Master's cause.

These various points, which I have run through rapidly, have taken a long time to read up, and I am principally indebted for my facts to a very excellent book written by a Methodist in America.*

I have in my hand a book called, *Memoirs of the Hymn Writers,* which has also been of some service to me; but a more bitter and scurrilous article than that upon Mr. John Wesley in this book I could not have conceived. After a person has exercised his judgment for a little while, he always begins to estimate an article upon a man by the general strain and current of it. Now, it was not sufficient for the writer of these *Memoirs of the Hymn Writers* simply to state the truth about Mr. Wesley, but there are not a few passages which commence with, " It is reported that he said." Now, there are enough sure and certain facts without quoting mere reports.

Although I am at the very antipodes of Mr. Wesley with regard to doctrinal views, I do not think it is at all fair to write an article against him in which his piety is suspected, and it is doubted whether he ever was a child of God at all. Of course, it is sheer bigotry that talks thus; and, instead of bringing facts against him, says, "It is reported that he said." Who among us could ever get to heaven, if we had to be judged by reports? Who could have a fair name among men if everything anybody likes to declare that we said should be taken as actual matter-of-fact ?

*   *   *   *   *   *

Charles Wesley has received among the ultra-Calvinists a better reputation than John, which he certainly does not deserve. Their doctrinal views were identical. I cannot detect any difference at all. Charles vacillated at different times, but he certainly had as great a hand in the Arminian controversy as John had, and I do not see any practical difference between the brothers. If one is good, so is

---

* See foot-note on page 28.

the other; and if one is bad, the other is bad, too; there is not much to choose between them. They both seem to me to have been very much mistaken, but they were earnest as far as their knowledge went.

Charles Wesley was a little younger than John. He was born in 1708. While a lad, the following remarkable circumstance occurred. A gentleman in Ireland, a Mr. Wellesley or Wesley, wished to adopt an heir, and he wrote to Mr. Samuel Wesley, the father, to know whether he had a son of the name of Charles; for, if he had, and was willing, the gentleman said he would adopt him, and make him his heir, leaving him all his large estates in Ireland. The father looked at it, and felt that the reply must be left to the discretion of his son. Charles decided to retain his own parentage and his own name, and not become the adopted son of another. Another person was chosen, who became the adopted son of this Mr. Wellesley or Wesley. He was the grandfather of the celebrated Marquis of Wellesley or Duke of Wellington. Strange circumstance this! We might not have had the Duke of Wellington to fight with Napoleon, we might not have had Mr. Charles Wesley as the earnest preacher, had he made another choice, and become the adopted son of this gentleman.

Charles was sent to Westminster School, and afterwards entered Christ Church College, Oxford. When his brother John first talked with him in Oxford about the things of God, his answer was, "What! would you have me become a saint all at once? Give me a little time to think about it." But he did become a saint all at once, after the fashion of his brother, seeking justification at first by works, just as blindly as Whitefield had done; for they were all blind at that time. Indeed, how could they be otherwise? They had no gospel teacher, and no sound Scriptural instruction.

Charles went by-and-by to Georgia with his brother, and he was appointed chaplain of the town of Frederica, 100 miles from Savannah. His experience there was about as sad as that of his brother John. He did not get on at all. The people at Frederica, on account of his faithful moral preaching, and his testimony against their vices, hated him, and tried to assassinate him. Once, when preaching, a pistol was fired at him : he happened at that moment to move, or else his valuable life would have been lost. They did not dare to make a second attempt at assassination, so they got up a trumpery accusation against him, through which he lost the confidence of the Governor, Mr. Oglethorpe, who then gave orders that Mr. Wesley was to use nothing that belonged to himself. Poor Wesley once asked for a few boards that he might lie on them, for he had to sleep on the damp ground, in a tent, even on cold wet nights, but they were refused him and given to another. He lay sick, and no one came to wait upon him. At last, two good women dared the anger of the Governor, and came to tend him.

A poor man died at the time in the colony, and at once Charles said he was well enough to get up, and he buried the body. He went home after the burial, and laid himself down upon the bedstead which had belonged to the poor man who had died ; but so great was the cruelty of the Governor, that he ordered the bedstead to be pulled from under him, and he was still left to lie at death's door without any medical advice, indeed, without any assistance except that which the two kind women I mentioned could give him.

John came over to see him, and Charles wanted to tell him about his sufferings. They talked together in Latin, which was very convenient, for the Governor forbade the two brothers conversing on the subject; but as those who were about could only hear the Latin, they, no doubt, thought they were both saying some Latin prayers. John

pleaded with the Governor, and the Governor restored
Charles to his favour, and then those people who had
been kicking and bullying him with all their might, came
round and beslavered him.   He began to despise men,
because they were so fickle ; for when he was out of favour
they scorned him, and when he was restored to the esteem
of the Governor, then, of course, they were at his feet,
and it was, " My dear sir, what can we do ?   Yours very
truly, and most obediently," and all that sort of thing.

He came home, and, like his brother John, he found
out that he had gone abroad to convert others and was
not converted himself; he, too, had been seeking the
way to heaven in his own strength and through his
own works, and found it was a hard road, and after all
did not lead to the desired haven, but conducted to the
chambers of despair.

How he found peace is very remarkable.   He had been
reading Law's *Serious Call to a Devout and Holy Life*, a
book which, I dare say, some of you have read.   He went to
see Mr. Law, who lived at Putney.   Disclosing his distress of
mind to him, Mr. Law, who knew nothing of the gospel,
gave Mr. Wesley some very good moral advice ; told
him to subdue self and to persevere in a course ot
mortification and subjection of the flesh, and so forth.
Such advice was of no use to his poor sin-sick soul.
He next went to see Count Zinzendorf, an incongruous
being, for he was a nobleman of wit, and a Bishop of
the Moravian Church—two strange things to be joined
together ; while Charles Wesley was equally incongruous,
for he was a High Churchman and yet a Methodist—two
very queer things also to be joined together.   These two
had a long conference about conversion.

Charles Wesley also talked with certain godly people about
the matter, and was very much shocked at their views ; such,
for instance, as that in a moment a man might be brought from

4

darkness to light, and from the power of Satan unto God. He read the *Life of Thomas Halyburton*, and that was greatly blessed to the enlightenment of his mind; but he did not find peace until a poor ignorant mechanic, ignorant only of earthly things, but well taught in the things of heaven, was the means of showing him more clearly the truth. This same mechanic, whose name was Bray, was the means of the conversion to God of Robert Ainsworth, who wrote the Latin Dictionary. When he was in his grey old age, this learned and mighty scholar came to sit at the feet of the poor humble mechanic like a child, to learn the way of salvation. This man is one whose name will never be written among the great ones of earth, but God greatly owned him in his little prayer-meetings to the conversion of such a man as Ainsworth, and to cheer the heart of such a man as Charles Wesley.

Wesley then read *Luther on the Galatians*, that precious book, which, containing the very marrow and fatness of the gospel, deals a death-blow to all legal righteousness, smiting all the works of the creature through the very heart, and making us feel we must go to God as sinners, to be saved through His sovereign mercy, through the atonement of Jesus Christ.

You will be astonished at the way in which Charles found perfect peace. He was very sick, lying very ill, and his soul was cast down within him. He knew the way of salvation, and knew that faith alone could save him; but he was like some of our own people, who say they cannot believe: he was troubled in mind, but did not feel that he could come to Christ. He thought himself unworthy and unfit; and as he lay there musing, he heard a voice, soft and solemn, speak to him, and the voice said, "In the name of Jesus of Nazareth, arise, and believe, and thou shalt be healed of thine infirmities, and thy sins shall be forgiven thee." Scarcely had the echo of the voice died away in the room, when light broke in upon his soul, peace glided into his mind, joy leaped into his heart. He gave utterance to his feelings in the following hymn, which he composed on the occasion :—

> "Long my imprison'd spirit lay,
>   Fast bound in sin and nature's night;
> Thine eye diffused a quickening ray;
>   I woke; the dungeon flamed with light;
> My chains fell off, my heart was free;
> I rose, went forth, and follow'd Thee.
>
> *   *   *   *   *
>
> "No condemnation now I dread;
>   Jesus, and all in Him, is mine:
> Alive in Him, my Living Head,
>   And, clothed with righteousness Divine,
> Bold I approach th' eternal throne,
> And claim the crown, through Christ, my own."

Perhaps two-thirds of you are saying, "Ah, that was a strange vision!" It was not a vision at all; it was a poor woman who had come in to clean the room, an illiterate but heavenly-minded woman. She had come imperceptibly into the room, and she glided out again as soon as she had uttered those words. She had heard his moaning, she had thought over his case, she had made it a matter of prayer, and it was impressed upon her mind to go and command him in the name of Jesus of Nazareth to rise and believe. And he did it; and this woman, through God, wrought this miracle of faith which set the bondaged soul free. When I read that, I thought, What an encouragement there is to me to preach to poor dead sinners, to go and say to poor souls that are dark, "Dark souls, be light;" for God, when we exercise faith in Him, gives us the same power as He gave to Peter, when he said to the lame man at the beautiful gate, "In the name of Jesus Christ of Nazareth rise up and walk," and he did so. It was not Peter's power, but it was the name of Jesus, that wrought the miracle. It was not this woman's word that blessed Wesley, but it was the power of her faith. Believing the name of Christ, she bade him believe, and thus he came to joy and peace and liberty.

And now you all know what Charles would want to do directly, he would want to—

> " Tell to sinners round
> What a dear Saviour he had found ; "

and he would want at once to—

> " Point to the Redeemer's blood,
> And say, ' Behold the way to God.' "

He did not feel that he could preach ; but when he was in a stage-coach, he began to talk to a lady who sat opposite ; and she, after she had heard him teach the doctrine of justification by faith, said she had half a mind to beat him for talking such blasphemy to her. On another occasion, a young man, a son of one of his dear friends, said, " Mr. Wesley, I am disgusted with your doctrine. Why, do you think the worst man or woman in the world will be equal to those of us who have been doing all we can these many years for religion ? Are these bad people to be saved the same way as we are ? I think that is a very wicked doctrine." He found that everywhere this precious truth met with the greatest possible opposition ; but what cared he about that ? It was his duty to preach it.

After a while, he obtained the curacy of Islington ; but after he had preached once or twice, the church-wardens would not let him preach, and though he appealed to the Bishop, yet they stood on the stairs and held the door fast, and said he should not preach. He tried it on once or twice ; but finding that he could by no means succeed, he went elsewhere.

While living in London, a clergyman came to ask him to preach a charity sermon at his church, a little way in the country. He went, and preached the gospel with great power, and the clergyman was so enraged with him that he struck him before the congregation. A good old farmer, an Essex man—I am always glad to say a word or two for my fellow-countrymen—came to him, and said, "Come and preach in my field, sir; nobody will hurt you there; at least, I will take care of them if they do." He had been preaching a sermon upon the new birth, and that touched the farmer's heart, and he said, "If that was what he preached, and the parson hit him for that, let him come and preach again," and so he did.

He once preached at Moorfields to ten thousand people, and at Kennington Common in the evening to twenty thousand. To get there, he rode across Lock's Fields, then unbuilt upon, and the owner, though he had done no hurt, summoned him for trespass and damages, and he was fined £20,—not for any damage he had done, but merely as a matter of spite, because he happened to be a Methodist.

On his way to Bristol he visited Gloucester, where George Whitefield was born. "The people of Gloucester desired to hear him preach. He sent to the minister of the parish to 'borrow his pulpit.' The minister politely sent back word that he should be happy at any time to take a glass of wine with him, but he dared not lend him his pulpit for fifty guineas." So Mr. Whitefield's brother, who kept the Bell Inn, said, "You shall preach in my field," and Mr. Wesley then and there preached to two thousand attentive hearers. Thus the field-preaching went on when the churches were shut against the Lord's servants; for the wide heaven and earth were always open for them.

He went down to Bristol, on one occasion, to preach, when bread was exceedingly dear. The poor people were all in excitement through the corn laws, and there was a great bread riot. A large body of people went rushing into Bristol, when Charles met them, and said, "What are you doing? What are you all after? What are you about?" "Oh," they said, "we must have bread!" "But," said he, "you can't get bread in this way;" upon which some of the ringleaders, who thought he might induce the people to turn back, came rushing up. He said to them, "Follow me," and he marched them to the schoolroom where he preached to them. While another band was getting to Kingswood, and doing mischief, he kept those miners under control, telling them they were more likely to get bread through praying to God than by plundering Bristol, and I believe it turned out that they were more successful.

He went through Wales, and preached where nearly all were Calvinists; but Charles was a very genial spirit, and he said, "I preach my own views, but I do not force them upon others." He once said, "I believe I could drive reprobation out of Wales in a year or two if I went there in a loving spirit." People have always represented that Calvinists preach reprobation, a doctrine we do not hold; it is not at all involved in election, but is a doctrine which we as much detest as the Arminians themselves do.

Charles did not escape persecution any more than the rest. On one occasion, he was arrested in the city of Cork, and prosecuted as a vagabond, because he went about doing good. What a blessed vagabond was our Lord Jesus Christ, who went about doing good from place to place! They soon set Mr. Charles free again; for they found there was little chance of laying hold of him legally. He said it was his deliberate opinion that the different riots and attacks that were made upon him and his brother were always incited by the clergy, and that the mob were not usually to blame. Why! this man preached two or three times a day, and the clergy only preached on Sunday morning, and never in the afternoon; they said they did not want to do double duty. Besides, people began to open their eyes, and a foxhunter, or a roaring singer, was not worthy of respect when he put on his gown. This made them hate the godly men, who had come forth to testify against their errors, and they therefore used any and every means to put them down.

Charles was more blessed than his brother John in his married life; indeed, he was exceedingly favoured. There was, at that time, at Garth in South Wales, a Mr. Gwynne, a magistrate, who was known by the name of "the King of Wales", because he had such great power. This gentleman determined to arrest Howell Harris, a friend of the Wesleys, for preaching; and if he had, he certainly would have put him in prison. He thought he would go and arrest him himself, so he went on horseback to the place where Harris was preaching. He stopped and listened to him for a short time, and thought it was not so very bad after all. He listened again, and it pleased God to prick him to the heart, and as he listened to the preaching, he found the Saviour. At the conclusion of the service he went up to Mr. Harris, and said, "Come home with me," and to the surprise of the crowd they saw Howell Harris ride off on his poor sorry nag side by side with the noble charger of Mr. Gwynne. They went home, and Mrs. Gwynne, who knew her husband had gone out to arrest Harris, saw him brought in with as much honour as if he had been the Archbishop of Canterbury.

Mrs. Gwynne thought her husband had gone mad, but her daughter Sarah did not think so. She, like her father, became deeply interested in the new doctrine, but her mother was greatly distressed at the turn affairs had taken. After a time, however, she ventured to hear Harris, and subsequently John Wesley when he visited Wales. She was delighted with him, and entertained him right royally.

Two years later, Charles Wesley arrived in Wales, on his way from Ireland, and stayed with the hospitable family.

" He was in very feeble health, being worn down by labour and exposure." After a brief rest at Garth, he felt able to resume his work for his Master, and he prepared for his return to London. Mr. Gwynne proposed to accompany his guest some way on the road. Mr. Wesley's horse was brought to the door with Mr. Gwynne's noble steed ; and there was Sarah, too, on her little pony. Soon the farewell words were spoken ; Mr. Wesley went on his way to London, but he could not forget Sarah Gwynne. He spoke to his brother John about his intention of proposing marriage to her, and I dare say John gave him good advice. He said he would do anything he could to aid him in it ; and this was to be the test whether it was to be a match or not ; if there was any objection raised, it should not be so. The question was asked, and the answer was given. Mr. Gwynne said he should be proud to have any relationship to one who bore the honoured name of Wesley ; and Mrs. Gwynne said that she should think it the happiest day in all her life on which she should be able to call a Wesley her son.

After Sarah Gwynne had become the wife of a Wesley, she, instead of being like the other, who stayed at home to revile, went with her husband on almost all his journeys, riding behind him on the horse many and many a weary mile ; walking with him, toiling with him, suffering with him, and bearing family afflictions by his side right cheerfully.

They had eight children. One died upon whom they had set their heart, and the mother's heart was sore stricken ; then the next died. The mother fell ill of the small-pox, and her face was much disfigured. Charles said, when she got well, she was more lovely in his eyes than ever before. Then another child died, and yet a fifth. Wesley went out to preach, and a lovely child whom he had left well was committed to the silent tomb ere he returned.

The mother's heart was broken, and she cried to God in her agony that he would at least spare some of her children.

It pleased God to spare two sons and a daughter. The daughter turned out well enough, but the sons were of no great account, and perhaps the mother's prayer had better never have been offered ; it might have been a mercy to have seen them carried to their graves. One became a Roman Catholic, and the other a moralist, but certainly nothing more than that.

Charles had not the ambition of his brother John, and at one time he did seem inclined to join Mr. Whitefield, and forsake his brother: Whitefield thought it would be a very unhallowed thing for the two brothers to be separated, and persuaded Charles to remain with his brother. He does not seem to have entered heartily into his brother's plan, though his brother at one time thought of making him his successor in his high office. I do not think Charles would have accepted the distinction. John had a bold and mighty thought before him; it was, to found a new denomination of which he should be the head, and which should bear his name ; with that design I do not think Charles had very much sympathy. He was sometimes, I think, rather a hindrance to his brother in his schemes than not. As for the doctrinal views of Charles, I have already told you that there is not much difference between those he entertained and those of his brother.

His hymns are, many of them, beautiful to the last degree ; he wrote nearly all the hymns in John Wesley's Hymn Book, and those in it which he did not compose are translations from the Moravian Hymn Book. Some of them are the richest hymns in any language, and express in the very noblest strains the utterance of the believer's heart. Let me just read you one or two of his hymns as specimens ; you have had one already, that hymn was composed when he was converted. He was in the habit of writing hymns in

the pulpit very frequently, and they were generally sug-
gested by the occasion. Of course, some of the hymns
were very poor, since he wrote so many ; his hymns would
have filled many volumes, but you have the cream of them
in the Wesleyan Hymn Book.

He was preaching at one time at Portland, where the
people were engaged in the stone quarries. He gave out
a hymn which he had just composed for the occasion :—

> " Come, O Thou all-victorious Lord !
> Thy power to us make known ;
> Strike with the hammer of Thy Word,
> And break these hearts of stone ! "

You may readily conceive with what enthusiasm that would
be sung in the midst of the stones. While at Newcastle,
observing the large fires kept in the collieries, illuminating
the heavens like a prairie-fire on the darkest night, he
composed the following hymn, to celebrate the spread of
the gospel.

> " See how great a flame aspires,
>   Kindled by a spark of grace !
> Jesu's love the nations fires,
>   Sets the kingdoms on a blaze :
> To bring fire on earth He came ;
>   Kindled in some hearts it is :
> Oh, that all might catch the flame,
>   All partake the glorious bliss !
>
> " When He first the work begun,
>   Small and feeble was His day ;
> Now the word doth swiftly run,
>   Now it wins its widening way :
> More and-more it spreads and grows,
>   Ever mighty to prevail,
> Sin's strongholds it now o'erthrows,
>   Shakes the trembling gates of hell."

Perhaps with a vivid imagination you can realize the soul-
stirring fervour with which those Newcastle miners would

roll out of their hoarse throats such a glorious hymn as that, with the fires blazing and shedding their lurid light upon their black cheeks. On one occasion, when one of his friends died, Mr. Charles Wesley stood by the bedside, and marked the spirit leave the clay, and as he stood there he composed and sang this hymn :—

" Ah, lovely appearance of death !
    No sight upon earth is so fair ;
Not all the gay pageants that breathe
    Can with a dead body compare :
With solemn delight I survey
    The corpse when the spirit is fled ;
In love with the beautiful clay,
    And longing to lie in its stead.

" How bless'd is our brother, bereft
    Of all that could burden his mind,
How easy the soul that has left
    This wearisome body behind !
Of evil incapable thou,
    Whose relics with envy I see,
No longer in misery now,
    No longer a sinner like me.

" This earth is affected no more
    With sickness, or shaken with pain :
The war in the members is o'er,
    And never shall vex him again :
No anger henceforward, or shame,
    Shall redden this innocent clay :
Extinct is the animal flame,
    And passion is vanish'd away.

"The languishing head is at rest,
    Its thinking and aching are o'er ;
The quiet immovable breast
    Is heaved by affliction no more :
The heart is no longer the seat
    Of trouble and torturing pain,
It ceases to flutter and beat,
    It never shall flutter again."

His funeral hymns were always considered by his brother to be the best that he wrote ; they were generally composed at the bed-side of the dying, or else at the graves of his friends. Finer hymns than some of these were never written by human hand, or sung by human voice. A few specimens will suffice ; they are well known to those who know the Methodist Hymn Book, but may not be known to you.

> "Oh ! what a mighty change
>   Shall Jesu's suff'rers know,
>   While o'er the happy plains they range,
>   Incapable of woe ! "

Once more, and what can excel this ?

> "And let this feeble body fail,
>   And let it droop, or die ;
>   My soul shall quit the mournful vale,
>   And soar to worlds on high ;
>   Shall join the disembodied saints,
>   And find its long-sought rest,
>   (That only bliss for which it pants,)
>   In my Redeemer's breast.
>
> "I bow me to my God's decree,
>   I own the sentence just,
>   (The sentence of mortality)
>   And dust returns to dust :
>   Yet quickened by the trumpet's sound,
>   This dust again shall rise,
>   Beyond the old creation bound,
>   And shine above the skies.
>
> "In hope of that immortal crown,
>   I now the cross sustain,
>   And gladly wander up and down,
>   And smile at toil and pain :
>   I suffer out my three-score years,
>   Till my Deliverer come,
>   And wipe away His servant's tears,
>   And take His exile home.

*   *   *   *

" Oh, what hath Jesus bought for me !
　　Before my ravish'd eyes
　Rivers of life Divine I see,
　　And trees of paradise :
　They flourish in perpetual bloom,
　　Fruit every month they give ;
　And to the healing leaves who come,
　　Eternally shall live.

" I see a world of spirits bright,
　　Who reap the pleasures there ;
　They all are robed in purest white,
　　And conquering palms they bear.
　Adorn'd by their Redeemer's grace
　　They close pursue the Lamb,
　And every shining front displays
　　Th' unutterable Name.

" Oh, what are all my sufferings here,
　　If, Lord, Thou count me meet
　With that enraptured host to appear,
　　And worship at Thy feet ?
　Give joy or grief, give ease or pain,
　　Take life or friends away :
　I come, to find them all again
　　In that eternal day."

One hymn very dear to us is of Charles Wesley's composition ; it is that well-known one,—

　　" Come, let us join our friends above
　　　Who have obtain'd the prize,
　　And on the eagle wings of love
　　　To joy celestial rise."

You know that touching part,—

　　" What numbers to their endless home
　　　This solemn moment fly ;
　　And we are to the margin come,
　　　And soon expect to die.

　　" E'en now by faith we join our hands
　　　With those that went before ;
　　And greet the blood-besprinkled bands
　　　On the eternal shore."

That hymn which is, if possible, still sweeter, is also his :—

> "Jesu, lover of my soul,
> Let me to Thy bosom fly."

Charles, you thus see, was the great poet of Methodism, while his brother was the great politician of it, and the framer of its rules. There are many interesting anecdotes connected with him, of which I will only give one or two. At Sheffield, a captain put a broadsword to his breast. Mr. Wesley unfastened his waistcoat and shirt, and bared his breast, saying, "Strike, sir, if you dare." After that, a man with a sickle stood ready to smite him, and would have killed him, but Charles Wesley cried out, "In the name of the Lord Jesus Christ, I command you to stand back!" and the man, abashed and confounded by the lion-like courage of Charles, slunk away into the crowd.

As for John and Charles Wesley, they seemed to fly with all the speed of seraphs,—they had never a moment's rest ; they were, from early in the morning till late at night, incessantly engaged in the good cause. As I have read their lives, and the lives of others, whom I hope to introduce to you on future occasions, I have felt as if I had not yet begun to live, and did not know how to begin. What have any of us done ? Oh ! these times need as much energy and fire as ever those times did ; there needs as much passion and earnestness for the conversion of men now as then ; there needs as much exertion that we may be good ministers of Christ, and clear our souls from the blood of men as in those olden times.

Is there not among us to-night a lion-like spirit, taught of God to know the value of his own soul and the preciousness of the Redeemer's blood? Is there not one man here who shall be anointed of the Holy Ghost to go forth and tell to others the way of salvation ? We do not lack for ministers, we have enough, such as they are ; but we do lack for ministers of a new kind, or rather of the old apostolic sort once more,—men whose hearts are a mass of molten metal, and whose tongues are like firebrands that have been kindled from the altar of the eternal God.

We have had some little specimens of revival through our land, but we have not had great and glorious shakings like those of that good time. Oh ! wherefore is it ? I am afraid that most of us are half asleep, and those that are a little awake have not begun to feel. It will be time for us to find fault with John and Charles Wesley, not when we discover their mistakes, but when we have cured our own. When we shall have more piety than they, more fire, more grace, more burning love, more intense unselfishness, then, and not till then, may we begin to find fault and criticize. For my part, I am as one who can see the spots in the sun, but know it to be the sun still, and only weep for my farthing candle by the side of such a luminary. It is far easier to discover those spots in the sun than it is to give forth his glory and light. Be it ours to remove such spots from ourselves by diligently searching God's Word, and by being built up and edified in our most holy faith.

Oh, remember, a dead creed is of no use, we must have our creed baptized with the Holy Ghost ; we must have love to God's truth, but there must be love to men's souls, too ! We must know what orthodoxy means, and we must not be heterodox in heart while we are orthodox in head. In the name of Him who lived and died for us, we must begin to wake up. The time past suffices us to have slept : the years that have gone over some of us are quite enough to have been spent in dilatoriness.

By that precious blood which once bedewed with sweat the brow of the Redeemer, and by that streaming gore which crimsoned His back ; by all the promises that are as yet unfulfilled, and the glorious hope of the Second

Advent, young men in the ministry, and you who are studying for it, ask God to help you to wake up. Preach not calmly and quietly as though you were asleep, but preach with fire and pathos and passion. And above all, preach, having prayed that the Holy Ghost will be with you; that the demonstration of the Spirit and His almighty power may be with your every word.

It will be a good day for the world when this College shall send out men of fire, and not for the world only, but for the church, and for heaven itself; as it shall be a joyful day when we send you brethren forth into the highways and hedges, the towns and the cities, compelling sinners to come in, that God's house may be filled and His table furnished with guests. The Lord grant it, for His name's sake! Amen.

77601323R00037

Made in the
USA
Columbia, SC